ANCIENT EGYPT

Virginia Loh-Hagan

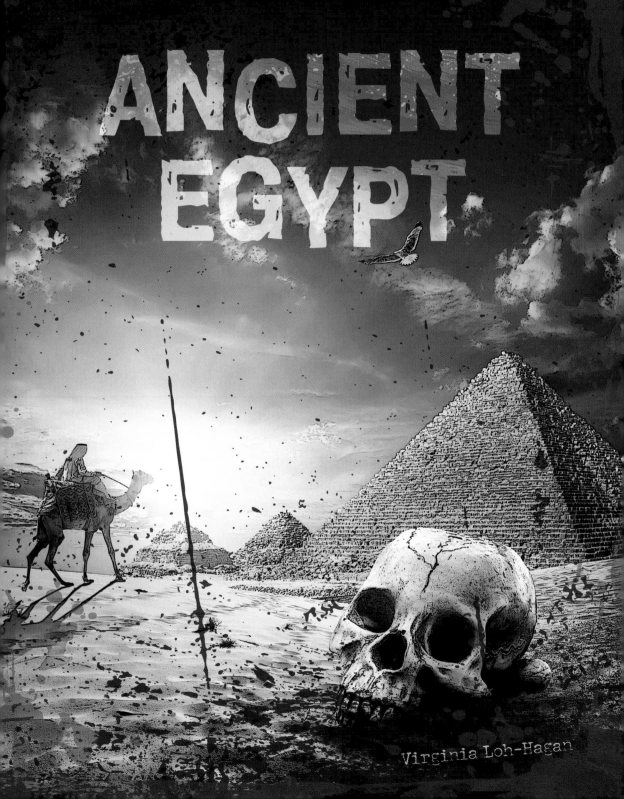

45TH PARALLEL PRESS

Published in the United States of America by Cherry Lake Publishing Group
Ann Arbor, Michigan
www.cherrylakepublishing.com
Reading Adviser: Marla Conn, MS, Ed., Literacy specialist, Read-Ability, Inc.

Book Designer: Melinda Millward

Photo Credits: © givaga/Shutterstock.com, cover, 1; © Guenter Albers/Shutterstock.com, 4; © Jose Ignacio Soto/Shutterstock.com, cover, 6; © Ewa Studio/Shutterstock.com, cover, 8; © Nastasic/ istockphoto.com, back cover, 10; © PhotocechCZ/Shutterstock.com, 12; © Margarita Soul Ray/ Shutterstock.com, 14; © Marzolino/Shutterstock.com, 16; © Robert Thom / Alamy Stock Photo 18; © De Luan / Alamy Stock Photo , 20; © Luisa Fumi/Shutterstock.com, 22; © Seqoya/Shutterstock.com, 24; © Maciek67/istockphoto.com, 27; © Instants/istockphoto.com, 28

Graphic Element Credits: © Milos Djapovic/Shutterstock.com, back cover, front cover; © cajoer/ Shutterstock.com, back cover, front cover, multiple interior pages; © GUSAK OLENA/Shutterstock.com, back cover, multiple interior pages; © Miloje/Shutterstock.com, front cover; © Rtstudio/Shutterstock. com, multiple interior pages; © Konstantin Nikiteev/Dreamstime.com, 29

Library of Congress Cataloging-in-Publication Data

Names: Loh-Hagan, Virginia, author.
Title: Ancient Egypt / by Virginia Loh-Hagan.
Description: Ann Arbor: Cherry Lake Publishing, [2021] | Series: Surviving history | Includes index.
Identifiers: LCCN 2020003325 (print) | LCCN 2020003326 (ebook) | ISBN 9781534169074 (hardcover)
  | ISBN 9781534170759 (paperback) | ISBN 9781534172593 (pdf) | ISBN 9781534174436 (ebook)
Subjects: LCSH: Egypt—History—To 332 B.C.—Juvenile literature. | Egypt—Civilization—Juvenile literature.
Classification: LCC DT83 .L77 2021 (print) | LCC DT83 (ebook) | DDC 932/.01—dc23
LC record available at https://lccn.loc.gov/2020003325
LC ebook record available at https://lccn.loc.gov/2020003326

Printed in the United States of America
Corporate Graphics

TABLE OF CONTENTS

INTRODUCTION

The Great Pyramid at Giza is 1 of the 7 wonders of the world.

Ancient Egypt is one of the oldest civilizations in the world. Ancient means from a time long ago. Ancient Egypt is in North Africa. The first ancient Egyptians were hunters and fishermen. They lived by the Nile River.

Ancient Egyptian history has 3 major periods. They did not follow directly after each other. The Old Kingdom lasted from approximately 2700 BCE to 2200 BCE. It had a strong central government. It's known as the age of **pyramids**. Pyramids are structures. They have a square base. They have sloping sides. The sides meet at a point. Ancient Egyptian pyramids served as tombs, or graves.

The Middle Kingdom lasted from approximately 2050 BCE to 1700 BCE. At this time, a strong army was built. Ancient Egypt was united under a **pharaoh**. Pharaohs were rulers at this time.

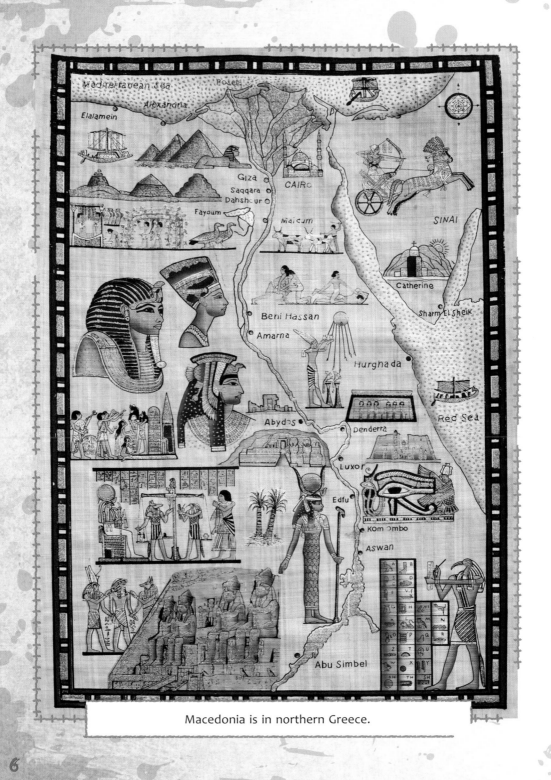

Macedonia is in northern Greece.

The New Kingdom lasted from approximately 1550 BCE to 1100 BCE. It's known as the golden age. Ancient Egyptians conquered lands. They expanded trade.

Ancient Egyptians thrived. They created a written language. They created a system of math. They created a religion of gods and goddesses. They created a system of medicine. They created building techniques. They created farming techniques. They created the first peace treaty.

But they also faced several dangers. A major danger was the **flooding** of the Nile. Flooding is when water overflows onto the land. Another danger was invasions. Alexander III of Macedon, also called Alexander the Great, conquered Egypt. Later, ancient Romans took over.

TO FLOOD OR NOT TO FLOOD?

The fertile area by the Nile is called black land.
It's only 5 percent of Egypt's land.

Egypt is a dry area. It doesn't get much rain. But the Nile River gave the area lots of water. There are floods every year. The Nile flooding made water spill onto the land. Water returned to the river. It left behind black **silt**. Silt was rich soil. This silt made the land **fertile**. Fertile means capable of growing food. The Nile River was also a major trade route.

The flooding brought life. Without floods, no food could grow. Without food, people **starved**. To starve is to die of hunger. But floods also brought death. Floods could be 30 feet (9 meters) aboveground. These floods destroyed villages. They drowned people. They drowned animals.

QUESTION 1

How did the **annual** Nile flooding affect you? Annual means yearly.

A You didn't live near the Nile River. This meant you were safe from floods. But it would've been hard for you to grow your own food. You had to trade for food.

B You were a priest or leader. You kept records of the Nile flooding. You knew when to escape. You used a **nilometer**. Nilometers are stone tablets. They had markings. These markings measured flood levels.

C You lived by the Nile River. You were there during the flooding season. This was May through August. You survived, but you had to rebuild your village each season.

Ancient Egyptians used the Nile flooding to tell time. They divided the year into 3 seasons: flooding, growing, and harvesting.

SURVIVAL TIPS

Follow these tips to survive a flood:

- Leave dangerous areas. Do this quickly. Leave everything behind. Go to a safe place.
- Move to higher ground. Move away from water. Get away from rivers. Get away from storm drains.
- Don't cross through water. Water up to your ankles can be dangerous. You can't see how deep the water is. A foot of water can make cars float.
- Bring a stick. Use it to measure water's depth. Use it to feel for the ground.
- Don't touch floodwater. The water is dirty. It could have germs. It could cause sicknesses.
- Turn over on your back if trapped in moving water. Swim backward. Use your feet to kick things out of the way. Find something to hold on to. Then, yell for help.

HIPPO OR HOME?

Hippos are no longer in Egypt.
But they did live in ancient Egypt.

The Nile River is home to many animals. Hippos were one of them. They're about 14 feet (4.3 m) long. They can weigh up to 8,000 pounds (3,629 kilograms). They run faster than humans. They have huge mouths. They have huge teeth. They can kill a human with a single bite.

In ancient Egypt, hippos killed people. They turned over fishing boats. They destroyed crops. They **stampeded**. Stampedes are when animals make a sudden rush. Ancient Egyptians feared hippos. But they also respected them.

King Tut was a pharaoh. Some experts think he was bitten by a hippo. Ancient Egyptians hunted hippos. They did this for sport. They used hippo meat, skin, and fat. They used hippo teeth to make art and weapons.

QUESTION 2

Would you have crossed paths with a hippo?

A You stayed home. You had no interest in messing with hippos. When you saw a hippo, you went the other way.

B You were an ancient Egyptian ruler. You hunted hippos. You did this to show your bravery and strength. You had help from your soldiers. You didn't hunt alone.

C You worked near the Nile. It was a part of the job. You had to be mindful of mother hippos and their babies. Hippos become **aggressive** when they feel danger. Aggressive means violent.

Hippos submerge themselves underwater. They look like land surrounded by water. Ancient Egyptians connected hippos to creation stories.

SURVIVAL BY THE NUMBERS

- Most ancient Egyptians didn't live past 40 years old.
- Ancient Egyptian civilization lasted about 3,000 years. That's over 10 times the age of the United States.
- Thutmose III was an ancient Egyptian pharaoh. He won a war. He was given "spoils of war." He got 340 prisoners of war. He got 1,796 servants.
- The pharaohs of the New Kingdom enslaved 250,000 people.
- Ancient Egyptians believed after death souls would confess their sins. About 42 ancient Egyptian gods listened to confessions.
- About 70 million mummies were made in ancient Egypt. Very few remain today.
- The Book of the Dead lists rules for how to live after death. It is 30 feet (9 m) long.
- In 2009, scientists studied the teeth of over 3,000 mummies. About 18 percent of mummies had dental diseases.

SICK OR HEALTHY?

Mosquitoes carry diseases. They're all around the Nile River.

The Nile River provided water and food. But it also brought sickness. There were **parasites** in the water. Parasites live on hosts. They feed on hosts.

Ancient Egyptians built **irrigation** channels. Irrigation is a system to supply water to land. The channels had standing water. Some ancient Egyptians waded through this water. Schistosoma worms were in the water. They're parasites. They entered human hosts. They laid eggs in their blood. They made people sick.

Some ancient Egyptians swallowed guinea worms. These worms were in drinking water. Female worms traveled through bodies. They laid eggs in the legs. This made people sick.

QUESTION 3

How likely were you to have gotten sick by worms?

 A You boiled all your water. You boiled your drinking water. You boiled your bathwater. You had to have time to boil water. You had to have money to make heat.

 B You avoided the river. You were a woman. You worked as a house servant. Or you were the lady of the house. Many ancient Egyptian women didn't work in the Nile River. They did more **domestic** work. Domestic means in the home.

C You were a working-class male. Ancient Egyptian men mostly worked in or by the Nile River.

Ancient Egyptians had the best doctors in the ancient world.

SURVIVOR BIOGRAPHY

Hatshepsut means "best of noble ladies." She was an ancient Egyptian pharaoh. She married her half-brother. She had a daughter. When her husband died, Hatshepsut became pharaoh. She was supposed to rule until her stepson came of age. But she took full power instead. She was 1 of at least 6 women to be pharaoh. She began her rule around 1479 BCE. She ruled until she was about 30 years old. She did many great things. She expanded trade. She built temples to the gods. She brought peace. She promoted the arts. In some pictures, she was painted as a male. She was painted with a beard. She was painted with big muscles. In other pictures, she was painted as a royal woman. When she died, her stepson became pharaoh. He hated Hatshepsut. He destroyed anything with her name and face. Her mummy was identified in 2007.

TOP OR BOTTOM OF THE PYRAMID?

A vizier is the pharaoh's master builder.
This person oversaw the work.

Building pyramids required a lot of workers. Most of the workers weren't **slaves**. Slaves are people who are forced to work without pay. Pyramids were mostly built by paid workers. These workers were a mix of skilled **craftsmen** and **laborers**. Craftsmen are people who can make things. They designed the pyramids. Laborers do physical work. They did the building.

Building pyramids was hard on the body. There were many accidents on work sites. Workers broke bones. They cracked skulls. They developed back problems. They developed **arthritis**. Arthritis is painful stiffness of joints.

Bits of sand and dirt were everywhere. These bits got into workers' eyes and lungs. This caused sickness.

QUESTION 4

Which role would you have played in building pyramids?

A You **surveyed** land. Survey means to assess areas. Surveyors chose building sites. They made plans. They also **excavated** areas. Excavate means to clear areas for building.

B You moved building materials. You mined rocks and stones. You brought them to the building site. You cut stones into blocks.

C You worked on building sites. You did all the heavy **labor**. Labor is work. You lifted. You hauled. You dug. You did anything that was needed. You followed orders.

Pyramid workers lived together. They lived in villages close to the building sites.

SURVIVAL TOOLS

Dams block water. Ancient Egyptians built the first known dam. They did this to control the Nile's flooding. They did this around 2950 to 2750 BCE. The dam is called Sadd el-Kafara. This means "Dam of the Infidels." Infidel is a person who doesn't follow the same religion. Sadd el-Kafara was made of stone walls. They built for 10 to 12 years. But it was never completed. It was destroyed by a flood. It was a gravity dam. It was made of stone bricks. It resisted water by its weight. Today, the Nile no longer floods. This is due to the Aswan Dam. The Aswan Dam was finished in 1971.

TO SERVE OR NOT TO SERVE?

Nomadic tribes lived around ancient Egypt. Nomadic means they moved around. Tribes are groups of people. They tried to settle in Egypt's fertile area.

The first ancient Egyptians thought Egypt was perfect. They weren't interested in other lands. They wanted to protect their own. Most of their wars were fought to unite their people. They also fought against invaders. Later, ancient Egyptians fought to gain lands.

Desert lands around Egypt helped protect it from invaders. But invaders still attacked. Ancient Egyptians built forts along the borders.

Soldier bodies were found in a tomb. They had head injuries. They had axe wounds. They had spear piercings. They had arrow cuts. Being a soldier was a tough life.

Akhenaten was a pharaoh. He didn't treat enemies well. Some stories say he **impaled** over 200 prisoners of war. Impale means to pierce a sharp pole through bodies.

QUESTION 5

What type of ancient Egyptian soldier would you have been?

A You were a **charioteer**. Charioteers drive **chariots**. Chariots were carts. They had wheels. They were pulled by horses. Charioteers were trained fighters. They were also rich. They bought their own equipment. Each chariot held 2 men: a driver and a fighter. Fighters had a bow, arrows, and a spear.

B You were an **archer**. Archers shot bows and arrows. You could shoot arrows over 600 feet (183 m). You killed enemies from afar.

C You were **infantry**. Infantry means a group of foot soldiers. You fought on the ground. You were the first to attack. You fought with spears. You fought with axes. You fought with short swords.

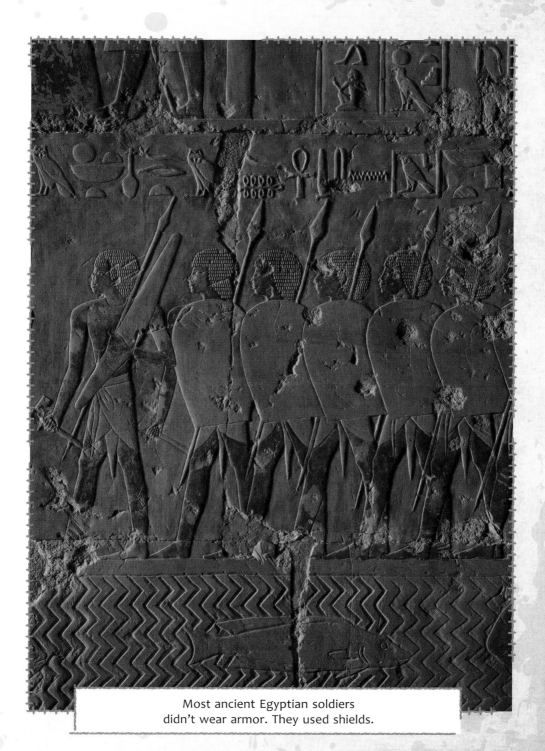

Most ancient Egyptian soldiers
didn't wear armor. They used shields.

SURVIVAL RESULTS

The pharaoh and his family were the most important people. They had their own doctors.

Would you have survived?

Find out! Add up your answers to the chapter questions. Did you have more **A**s, **B**s, or **C**s?

- If you had more **A**s, then you're a survivor! Congrats!

- If you had more **B**s, then you're on the edge. With some luck, you might have just made it.

- If you had more **C**s, then you wouldn't have survived.

Are you happy with your results? Did you have a tie? Sometimes fate is already decided for us. Follow the link below to our webpage. Scroll until you find the series name *Surviving History*. Click download. Print out the template. Follow the directions to create your own paper die. Read the book again. Roll the die to find your new answers. Did your fate change?

https://cherrylakepublishing.com/teaching_guides

DIGGING DEEPER: DID YOU KNOW...?

Ancient Egypt was exciting. People achieved great things. But many lives were lost as well. Surviving history involves many different factors. Dig deeper. Consider some of the facts below.

QUESTION 1:

How did the annual Nile flooding affect you?

- Outside of the Nile is the red land. These are desert lands.
- Nilometers were built in temples.
- About 95 percent of Egyptians live close to the river.

QUESTION 2:

Would you have crossed paths with a hippo?

- Hippos roar in the morning. They roar at night. Ancient Egyptians thought they were saying hello and good-bye to the sun.
- Rulers killing hippos showed victory over disorder.
- Soldiers captured hippos. Rulers pretended to hunt them for show.

QUESTION 3:

How likely were you to have gotten sick by worms?

- Ancient Egyptians used water bowls at mealtimes. They dipped their hands in water. They used their hands to eat.
- Ancient Egyptian women had more rights than other civilizations. They could own land. They could have jobs.
- Most ancient Egyptian men worked in farming.

QUESTION 4:

Which role would you have played in building pyramids?

- Ancient Egyptians believed in "bak." This meant everyone owed service to someone above them in society.
- Wheels wouldn't have worked in sand. So, workers pulled the stones instead.
- Workers were split into crews. They worked in shifts. This spread out the workload. It got the work done faster.

QUESTION 5:

What type of ancient Egyptian soldier would you have been?

- Charioteers had a high social status. They were fast. They could move easily. They were powerful.
- Rich people hunted. So, they had archery skills.
- Most soldiers were from lower classes. They had little training. Only men became soldiers.

GLOSSARY

aggressive (uh-GRES-iv) hostile and violent
ancient (AYN-shuhnt) from a time long ago
annual (AN-yoo-uhl) yearly
archer (AHR-chur) a person who shoots with a bow and arrows
arthritis (ahr-THRYE-tis) painful stiffness or inflammation of joints
charioteer (char-ee-uh-TEER) a person who fights on a chariot
chariots (CHAR-ee-uhts) wheeled carts pulled by large animals
craftsmen (KRAFTS-men) skilled workers who can make things
domestic (duh-MES-tik) housework
excavated (EK-skuh-vay-tid) cleared land for use
fertile (FUR-tuhl) capable of growing food
flooding (FLUHD-ing) water overflowing
impaled (im-PAYLD) pierced a sharp pole through bodies

infantry (IN-fuhn-tree) foot soldiers
irrigation (ir-uh-GAY-shun) system to supply water to land
labor (LAY-bur) work
laborers (LAY-bur-urz) manual workers
nilometer (NYE-luh-mee-ter) stone tablet with markings that measure flood levels
nomadic (noh-MAD-ik) to move from place to place
parasites (PAR-uh-sites) organisms that live on hosts
pharaoh (FAIR-oh) ancient Egyptian ruler
pyramids (PIR-uh-midz) structures with a square base and sloping sides that meet in a point at the top
silt (SILT) rich soil
slaves (SLAYVZ) people who are forced to work for free
stampeded (stam-PEE-did) sudden rush by large animals
starved (STAHRVD) died of hunger
surveyed (SUR-vayd) assessed or evaluated an area for use
tribes (TRYBZ) groups of people

LEARN MORE!

- Carr, Simonetta. *Cleopatra and Ancient Egypt for Kids: Her Life and World, with 21 Activities.* Chicago, IL: Chicago Review Press, 2018.
- Jennings, Ken, and Mike Lowery (illust.). *Ancient Egypt.* New York, NY: Little Simon, 2015.
- Napoli, Donna Jo, and Christina Balit (illust.). *Treasury of Egyptian Mythology: Classic Stories of Gods, Goddesses, Monsters, and Mortals.* Washington, DC: National Geographic, 2013.

INDEX

ABOUT THE AUTHOR

Dr. Virginia Loh-Hagan is an author, university professor, and former classroom teacher. She wrote a 45th Parallel Press series about ancient Egyptian gods and goddesses. She lives in San Diego with her very tall husband and very naughty dogs. To learn more about her, visit www.virginialoh.com.